55 Brazilian Recipes for Home

By: Kelly Johnson

Table of Contents

- Feijoada
- Moqueca de Peixe
- Pão de Queijo
- Brigadeiro
- Coxinha
- Acarajé
- Vatapá
- Caipirinha
- Quindim
- Farofa
- Bobó de Camarão
- Baião de Dois
- Tapioca Crepes
- Canjica
- Caldo Verde
- Churrasco
- Carne de Sol
- Cuscuz Paulista
- Arroz de Carreteiro
- Pacu Assado
- Xinxim de Galinha
- Buchada de Bode
- Rabada
- Sarapatel
- Beijinho
- Cuscuz Branco
- Linguiça Mineira
- Tutu de Feijão
- Manjar Branco
- Cocada
- Pé-de-Moleque
- Arroz Doce
- Canjiquinha
- Escondidinho
- Frango com Quiabo

- Quibebe
- Doce de Abóbora
- Arroz Carreteiro
- Virado à Paulista
- Bolinho de Bacalhau
- Arroz de Forno
- Ensopado de Borrego
- Mocotó
- Frango à Passarinho
- Angu à Baiana
- Empadão Goiano
- Pastel
- Sagu de Vinho
- Maria Isabel
- Cocido Brasileño
- Dobradinha
- Canjica Nordestina
- Caruru
- Canjica com Amendoim
- Bolo de Rolo

Feijoada

Ingredients:

- 1 lb black beans, soaked overnight
- 1/2 lb pork shoulder, diced
- 1/2 lb smoked sausage, sliced
- 1/2 lb bacon, chopped
- 2 onions, chopped
- 4 cloves garlic, minced
- 2 bay leaves
- Salt and pepper to taste
- Water for cooking

Instructions:

Rinse the soaked black beans and place them in a large pot. Cover with water and cook until the beans are tender. This can take 1-2 hours, depending on the beans.

In a separate pan, cook the bacon until it becomes crispy. Add the chopped onions and minced garlic, sautéing until the onions are translucent.

Add the diced pork shoulder and sliced smoked sausage to the pan. Cook until the meats are browned.

Transfer the meat mixture to the pot with the cooked black beans. Add bay leaves, salt, and pepper to taste.

Simmer the feijoada on low heat for about an hour, allowing the flavors to meld together. If needed, add more water to achieve your desired consistency.

Adjust seasoning to taste and continue simmering until the meat is tender.

Serve the feijoada hot over white rice, accompanied by orange slices and greens (such as collard greens or kale).

Note: Traditional feijoada may include other cuts of meat like pork ribs, sausage, and even beef. Feel free to customize the recipe based on your preferences. Enjoy your Brazilian feast!

Moqueca de Peixe

Ingredients:

- 1.5 lbs white fish fillets (snapper, cod, or another firm white fish)
- 1 onion, sliced
- 1 bell pepper, sliced
- 2 tomatoes, chopped
- 2 cloves garlic, minced
- 1 cup coconut milk
- 1 tbsp palm oil
- 1 lime, juiced
- Salt and pepper to taste
- Fresh cilantro for garnish

Instructions:

Marinate the fish fillets with lime juice, salt, and pepper. Let them sit for about 15-20 minutes.
In a large, deep pan, heat the palm oil over medium heat. Add the minced garlic and sauté until fragrant.
Add the sliced onions and bell peppers to the pan. Sauté until the vegetables are softened.
Stir in the chopped tomatoes and cook until they release their juices.
Place the marinated fish fillets on top of the vegetables in the pan.
Pour in the coconut milk, ensuring it covers the fish and vegetables.
Cover the pan and let the moqueca simmer over medium-low heat for about 15-20 minutes, or until the fish is cooked through.
Season with additional salt and pepper to taste.
Garnish with fresh cilantro before serving.
Serve the Moqueca de Peixe over white rice or with crusty bread to soak up the delicious broth.

Enjoy this flavorful and comforting Brazilian fish stew!

Pão de Queijo

Ingredients:

- 2 cups tapioca flour
- 1 cup milk
- 1/2 cup butter
- 1 tsp salt
- 1 1/2 cups grated Parmesan cheese
- 2 beaten eggs

Instructions:

Preheat your oven to 375°F (190°C) and grease a mini muffin tin.

In a saucepan, combine the milk, butter, and salt. Bring it to a boil, stirring to ensure the butter is fully melted.

Place the tapioca flour in a large mixing bowl. Pour the hot milk mixture over the tapioca flour and stir well until the mixture is well combined. Allow it to cool slightly.

Once the mixture has cooled a bit, add the grated Parmesan cheese and beaten eggs. Mix until you have a smooth batter.

Spoon the batter into the mini muffin tin, filling each cup almost to the top.

Bake in the preheated oven for about 15-20 minutes or until the tops of the cheese bread are lightly golden.

Allow the Pão de Queijo to cool for a few minutes before removing them from the muffin tin.

Serve them warm and enjoy these delightful, cheesy Brazilian treats!

Note: Pão de Queijo is often enjoyed with coffee or as a snack. The outside is crispy, and the inside is soft and chewy with a cheesy flavor.

Brigadeiro

Ingredients:

- 1 can (14 oz) sweetened condensed milk
- 2 tbsp unsweetened cocoa powder
- 2 tbsp unsalted butter
- Chocolate sprinkles for coating

Instructions:

In a medium-sized saucepan, combine the sweetened condensed milk, cocoa powder, and butter.

Cook the mixture over medium heat, stirring constantly to avoid burning, until it thickens and starts to pull away from the sides of the pan. This usually takes about 10-15 minutes.

Once the mixture has thickened and reaches a fudgy consistency, remove it from the heat. Let it cool for a few minutes until it's easy to handle.

Grease your hands with butter to prevent sticking, then take small portions of the mixture and roll them into bite-sized balls.

Roll each Brigadeiro ball in chocolate sprinkles until fully coated.

Place the Brigadeiros on a plate or in mini cupcake liners.

Let them cool completely before serving.

Brigadeiros are rich, fudgy, and intensely chocolatey. They are a favorite treat in Brazil and are often present at birthday parties and other festive occasions. Enjoy!

Coxinha

Ingredients:

For the Chicken Filling:

- 1 lb boneless, skinless chicken breasts
- 1 onion, finely chopped
- 2 cloves garlic, minced
- Salt and pepper to taste
- 1 bay leaf
- 1 cup chicken broth
- 2 tablespoons olive oil
- 1/2 cup cream cheese (optional)

For the Dough:

- 2 cups chicken broth
- 2 tablespoons unsalted butter
- 2 cups all-purpose flour
- Salt to taste

For Coating and Frying:

- 2 cups breadcrumbs
- 2 eggs, beaten
- Oil for deep frying

Instructions:

Chicken Filling:

In a pot, combine chicken breasts, onion, garlic, salt, pepper, bay leaf, and chicken broth.
Simmer until the chicken is cooked and easily shredded. Shred the chicken.

Dough:

In a separate pot, combine chicken broth, butter, and salt. Bring to a boil.

Add the flour all at once, stirring constantly until a dough forms and pulls away from the sides of the pot.
Allow the dough to cool slightly.

Assembling Coxinhas:

Take a small portion of the dough, flatten it in your hand, and place a spoonful of the shredded chicken in the center.
Add a small amount of cream cheese if desired.
Encase the filling with the dough, forming a teardrop or drumstick shape.
Dip each coxinha in beaten eggs, then coat it with breadcrumbs.

Frying:

Heat oil in a deep fryer or deep pan to 350°F (175°C).
Fry the coxinhas until they are golden brown and crispy.
Remove from oil and place them on a paper towel to absorb excess oil.

Serve coxinhas hot as a delicious snack or appetizer. Enjoy!

Acarajé

Ingredients:

For the Acarajé Dough:

- 2 cups dried black-eyed peas, soaked overnight
- 1 small onion, finely chopped
- 2 cloves garlic, minced
- Salt to taste
- Vegetable oil for frying

For the Filling:

- Dried shrimp, soaked
- Caruru (a traditional okra and shrimp stew)
- Vatapá (a spicy mixture of bread, shrimp, coconut milk, and peanuts)
- Sliced tomatoes
- Hot sauce (optional)

Instructions:

For the Acarajé Dough:

Drain and rinse the soaked black-eyed peas. In a food processor, blend the peas with the chopped onion, minced garlic, and salt until you get a smooth, thick batter.
Heat vegetable oil in a deep fryer or a heavy-bottomed pot to 350°F (175°C).

Forming and Frying:

Wet your hands and scoop out a small portion of the batter.
Flatten the batter in your palm and form a small well in the center.
Drop the formed dough into the hot oil and fry until golden brown, turning occasionally for even cooking.
Remove the acarajé from the oil and drain excess oil on paper towels.

Assembling:

Slice open the fried acarajé horizontally, creating a pocket.

Fill the pocket with a mixture of dried shrimp, caruru, vatapá, sliced tomatoes, and hot sauce if desired.

Acarajé is often served as a street food delicacy, and its unique combination of flavors makes it a delightful experience. Enjoy this taste of Bahia!

Vatapá

Ingredients:

- 2 cups dried shrimp, soaked in water
- 2 cups unsalted roasted peanuts, ground
- 2 cups bread, torn into small pieces
- 1 cup coconut milk
- 1 onion, chopped
- 2 cloves garlic, minced
- 2 tbsp dendê oil (palm oil)
- 1 cup fish or shrimp broth (from soaking the dried shrimp)
- Salt and pepper to taste

Instructions:

Soak Dried Shrimp:
- Place dried shrimp in a bowl and cover with warm water. Let them soak for about 30 minutes.

Prepare Ingredients:
- After soaking, drain the dried shrimp and reserve the liquid.
- In a blender or food processor, combine soaked dried shrimp, ground peanuts, torn bread, coconut milk, and fish or shrimp broth. Blend until you get a smooth paste.

Cook Vatapá:
- In a large pan, heat dendê oil over medium heat.
- Add chopped onions and minced garlic. Sauté until the onions are soft and translucent.

Combine Ingredients:
- Pour the blended paste into the pan with sautéed onions and garlic. Stir continuously to avoid lumps.
- Cook the mixture over low to medium heat, stirring constantly until it thickens. This may take about 15-20 minutes.

Season and Serve:
- Season the vatapá with salt and pepper to taste.
- Continue cooking until the mixture reaches a creamy consistency.

Vatapá is now ready to be used as a delicious filling for Acarajé or served alongside rice. The combination of flavors from the shrimp, peanuts, and coconut milk gives Vatapá a unique and delightful taste. Enjoy!

Caipirinha

Ingredients:

- 2 oz (60 ml) cachaça
- 1 lime, cut into wedges
- 2 teaspoons sugar (adjust to taste)
- Ice cubes

Instructions:

Prepare the Lime:
- Cut the lime into wedges or slices. Remove the ends and any seeds.

Muddle the Lime:
- Place the lime wedges in a glass.
- Sprinkle sugar over the lime wedges.
- Using a muddler or the back of a spoon, gently muddle (press and crush) the lime and sugar together. Be careful not to over-muddle and release bitter compounds from the lime peel.

Add Cachaça:
- Pour the cachaça over the muddled lime and sugar.

Mix and Chill:
- Stir the mixture to dissolve the sugar and blend the flavors.
- Add ice cubes to the glass to chill the drink.

Serve:
- Optionally, you can garnish the Caipirinha with an additional lime wedge.

Enjoy:
- Stir the drink occasionally as you enjoy its refreshing taste.

Note: Some variations include using different fruits such as strawberries or passion fruit, but the classic Caipirinha is made with lime.

Caipirinha is a delightful cocktail that perfectly captures the spirit of Brazil. It's a popular choice for warm days and festive occasions. Cheers!

Quindim

Ingredients:

- 2 cups sweetened shredded coconut
- 1 cup granulated sugar
- 4 large egg yolks
- 1/4 cup unsalted butter, melted
- 1/4 cup coconut milk (or regular milk)
- 1 teaspoon vanilla extract
- Pinch of salt

Instructions:

Preheat the Oven:
- Preheat your oven to 350°F (175°C). Grease a muffin tin or use individual fluted molds.

Prepare Coconut:
- In a food processor, pulse the sweetened shredded coconut until it becomes finer in texture.

Mix Ingredients:
- In a large bowl, combine the pulsed coconut, granulated sugar, egg yolks, melted butter, coconut milk, vanilla extract, and a pinch of salt. Mix well until the ingredients are thoroughly combined.

Fill Molds:
- Spoon the mixture into the greased molds, pressing it down gently.

Bake:
- Place the molds in the preheated oven and bake for approximately 20-25 minutes or until the tops are golden and a toothpick inserted into the center comes out clean.

Cool:
- Allow the Quindim to cool in the molds for a few minutes before transferring them to a wire rack to cool completely.

Serve:
- Once cooled, gently remove the Quindim from the molds. They are traditionally served at room temperature.

Quindim has a rich, custard-like texture and a sweet coconut flavor. It's a popular dessert in Brazil and often enjoyed during celebrations. Enjoy your homemade Quindim!

Farofa

Ingredients:

- 1 cup cassava flour (farinha de mandioca)
- 2 tablespoons vegetable oil or butter
- 1 onion, finely chopped
- 2 cloves garlic, minced
- Salt and pepper to taste
- Optional additions: chopped bacon, sausage, eggs, olives, raisins, or finely chopped vegetables like carrots and bell peppers.

Instructions:

Prepare Ingredients:
- If using any optional additions like bacon or sausage, cook them in a pan until they are browned and crispy. Set aside.

Saute Onions and Garlic:
- In a large skillet, heat the vegetable oil or butter over medium heat. Add the finely chopped onion and minced garlic. Sauté until the onions are translucent.

Add Cassava Flour:
- Add the cassava flour to the skillet. Stir well to combine it with the onions and garlic. Cook over medium heat, stirring frequently, until the cassava flour is toasted and turns a golden brown color. This usually takes about 5-8 minutes.

Incorporate Optional Ingredients:
- If using any optional additions, such as bacon or sausage, add them back to the skillet. Mix well.

Season:
- Season the farofa with salt and pepper to taste. Adjust the seasoning according to your preferences.

Serve:
- Remove the farofa from the heat and let it cool slightly before serving.

Farofa adds a delightful crunchy texture and a unique flavor to meals. It pairs well with various Brazilian dishes, especially barbecue and stews. Enjoy your Farofa as a tasty and versatile side dish!

Bobó de Camarão

Ingredients:

For the Cassava Puree:

- 1 lb cassava (yuca), peeled and chopped
- Water for boiling
- Salt to taste

For the Shrimp and Sauce:

- 1.5 lbs large shrimp, peeled and deveined
- 1 onion, finely chopped
- 2 cloves garlic, minced
- 1 red bell pepper, chopped
- 1 green bell pepper, chopped
- 1 can (14 oz) coconut milk
- 2 tablespoons dendê oil (palm oil)
- 2 tablespoons olive oil
- 1 tablespoon tomato paste
- 1 tablespoon fresh cilantro, chopped
- Salt and pepper to taste
- Lime wedges for serving

Instructions:

For the Cassava Puree:

>Place the chopped cassava in a pot, cover with water, and add salt.
>Boil until the cassava is tender (about 15-20 minutes). Drain the water.
>Mash the cooked cassava or blend it in a food processor until you get a smooth puree. Set aside.

For the Shrimp and Sauce:

>In a large pan, heat olive oil and dendê oil over medium heat.
>Sauté the chopped onion and minced garlic until softened.
>Add the red and green bell peppers, sautéing until they are tender.
>Stir in the tomato paste and cook for a couple of minutes.

Pour in the coconut milk and bring the mixture to a simmer.
Add the shrimp to the pan and cook until they turn pink and are cooked through.
Gently fold in the cassava puree, stirring until the sauce thickens and the ingredients are well combined.
Season with salt and pepper to taste. Adjust the seasoning if needed.
Sprinkle fresh cilantro over the Bobó de Camarão before serving.
Serve the Bobó de Camarão over rice and with lime wedges on the side.

Bobó de Camarão is a delightful dish that showcases the rich flavors of Brazilian cuisine, combining the creaminess of cassava with the succulence of shrimp. Enjoy!

Baião de Dois

Ingredients:

- 1 lb large shrimp, peeled and deveined
- 1 onion, finely chopped
- 3 cloves garlic, minced
- 1 red bell pepper, chopped
- 1 green bell pepper, chopped
- 2 tomatoes, chopped
- 1 cup coconut milk
- 2 tablespoons dende oil (palm oil)
- 1 cup chicken or seafood broth
- 2 tablespoons tomato paste
- 2 tablespoons cilantro, chopped
- 2 tablespoons green onions, chopped
- Salt and pepper to taste
- Lime wedges for serving
- Cooked white rice for serving

Instructions:

Prepare Shrimp:
- Season the shrimp with salt and pepper. Set aside.

Sauté Aromatics:
- In a large pan, heat the dende oil over medium heat. Add the chopped onion and garlic. Sauté until softened.

Add Vegetables:
- Add the chopped red and green bell peppers to the pan. Cook until the vegetables are tender.

Incorporate Tomatoes and Tomato Paste:
- Add the chopped tomatoes and tomato paste to the pan. Stir well and cook until the tomatoes break down.

Cook Shrimp:
- Add the seasoned shrimp to the pan. Cook for a few minutes until the shrimp turn pink and opaque.

Pour Coconut Milk and Broth:

- Pour in the coconut milk and chicken or seafood broth. Stir to combine all the ingredients.

Simmer and Season:
- Let the mixture simmer for about 10-15 minutes, allowing the flavors to meld. Season with salt and pepper to taste.

Finish with Herbs:
- Stir in chopped cilantro and green onions.

Serve:
- Serve the Bobó de Camarão over cooked white rice. Garnish with additional cilantro and green onions. Serve with lime wedges on the side.

Bobó de Camarão is a rich and comforting dish, perfect for seafood lovers. Enjoy the vibrant flavors of Brazilian cuisine!

Tapioca Crepes

Ingredients:

- 1 cup tapioca flour (also known as tapioca starch or polvilho)
- 1/2 cup water
- Pinch of salt
- Optional fillings: cheese, ham, coconut, chocolate, condensed milk, etc.

Instructions:

Prepare the Tapioca Flour:
- In a mixing bowl, combine the tapioca flour and a pinch of salt.

Add Water:
- Gradually add water to the tapioca flour while stirring continuously. Continue mixing until you achieve a smooth, lump-free batter.

Rest the Batter:
- Allow the batter to rest for about 15-20 minutes. This helps the tapioca granules absorb the water, resulting in a better consistency.

Heat the Pan:
- Heat a non-stick skillet or crepe pan over medium heat.

Cook the Crepes:
- Pour a thin layer of the tapioca batter onto the hot skillet, spreading it evenly to form a circular shape.
- Cook until the edges start to lift and the bottom is lightly golden. Tapioca crepes cook relatively quickly, usually in 1-2 minutes.
- Flip the crepe and cook briefly on the other side until it's set.

Add Fillings:
- If desired, add your choice of fillings to one half of the crepe while it's still in the pan. Popular fillings include grated cheese, ham, coconut, chocolate, or condensed milk.

Fold and Serve:
- Fold the crepe in half, covering the fillings, and then transfer it to a plate.
- Serve the tapioca crepes warm and enjoy!

Tapioca crepes are versatile and can be adapted to both sweet and savory preferences. They are a staple street food in Brazil and are commonly enjoyed for breakfast or as a snack. Feel free to experiment with different fillings to suit your taste.

Canjica

Ingredients:

- 1 cup canjica (dried hominy corn)
- Water for soaking
- 1 cinnamon stick
- 4 cups whole milk
- 1 cup sugar
- Condensed milk (optional, for serving)
- Cinnamon powder (optional, for serving)

Instructions:

Soak the Canjica:
- Rinse the canjica under cold water, then soak it in water overnight or for at least 8 hours. This helps soften the corn kernels.

Cook the Canjica:
- Drain the soaked canjica and place it in a large pot with enough water to cover. Add a cinnamon stick to the pot.
- Bring the canjica to a boil, then reduce the heat to a simmer. Cook until the corn is tender. This may take about 1 to 1.5 hours, depending on the type of canjica you have.

Add Milk and Sugar:
- Once the canjica is tender, add the whole milk and sugar to the pot.
- Continue cooking over medium heat, stirring frequently to prevent sticking, until the mixture thickens. This may take another 30 minutes.

Serve:
- Once the canjica has reached the desired consistency, remove the cinnamon stick.
- Serve the canjica warm in individual bowls.

Optional Toppings:
- Drizzle condensed milk on top for extra sweetness.
- Sprinkle cinnamon powder over each serving.

Canjica is a comforting and delicious dessert, often associated with Brazilian cultural celebrations. It can be enjoyed both warm and cold, making it a versatile treat for various occasions.

Caldo Verde

Ingredients:

- 3 large potatoes, peeled and diced
- 1 onion, finely chopped
- 3 cloves garlic, minced
- 2 tablespoons olive oil
- 1 chorizo or linguica sausage, sliced
- 6 cups chicken or vegetable broth
- 1 bunch kale, stems removed and leaves thinly sliced
- Salt and pepper to taste

Instructions:

Prepare Vegetables:
- Peel and dice the potatoes, finely chop the onion, and mince the garlic.

Sauté Onions and Garlic:
- In a large pot, heat olive oil over medium heat. Add chopped onions and minced garlic. Sauté until the onions are translucent.

Add Potatoes and Sausage:
- Add the diced potatoes to the pot and continue to sauté for a few minutes. Then, add the sliced chorizo or linguica sausage and cook until the sausage is browned.

Pour in Broth:
- Pour in the chicken or vegetable broth. Bring the mixture to a boil and then reduce the heat to a simmer. Cook until the potatoes are tender.

Blend:
- Use an immersion blender to partially blend the soup, leaving some chunks of potatoes for texture. If you don't have an immersion blender, transfer a portion of the soup to a blender, blend, and then return it to the pot.

Add Kale:
- Add the thinly sliced kale to the pot. Simmer until the kale is tender, which usually takes about 5-10 minutes.

Season:
- Season the soup with salt and pepper to taste.

Serve:
- Ladle the Caldo Verde into bowls and serve hot.

Caldo Verde is often enjoyed with a drizzle of olive oil on top. It's a nutritious and flavorful soup that is popular in both Portuguese and Brazilian cuisines.

Churrasco

Ingredients:

For the Meat:

- Beef cuts such as picanha (rump cap), sirloin, ribeye, and flank steak
- Chicken wings or thighs
- Pork sausages (linguica)
- Salt to taste

For the Marinade (optional):

- Olive oil
- Garlic cloves, minced
- Fresh parsley, chopped
- Salt and pepper to taste

For Serving:

- Farofa (toasted cassava flour)
- Chimichurri sauce (a condiment made with parsley, garlic, vinegar, oil, and red pepper flakes)

Instructions:

Prepare the Meat:
- If you're using large cuts of beef, such as picanha, trim excess fat and score the fat cap. Cut the meat into skewer-sized portions.

Marinate the Meat (Optional):
- If desired, marinate the meat with a mixture of olive oil, minced garlic, chopped parsley, salt, and pepper. Allow it to marinate for at least 30 minutes to enhance the flavor.

Prepare the Grill:
- Heat your charcoal or gas grill to medium-high heat.

Grilling:
- Place the meat on the grill, starting with the larger cuts first. Cook each side to your desired doneness.
- For picanha, grill the fat cap side first to render some of the fat. Then, cook the other sides to your liking.

- Grill chicken wings or thighs until fully cooked and slightly charred.
- Grill pork sausages until they are browned and cooked through.

Resting:
- Allow the grilled meat to rest for a few minutes before serving to retain juices.

Serve:
- Serve the churrasco with sides like farofa and chimichurri sauce.

Churrasco is a social and festive way of cooking and enjoying a variety of meats. It's often a centerpiece at gatherings and celebrations in Brazil, bringing people together around the grill. Adjust the seasoning and choice of meats according to your preferences. Enjoy your Brazilian churrasco!

Carne de Sol

Ingredients:

- 2 to 3 pounds of beef (common cuts include round, sirloin, or brisket)
- Coarse salt
- Black pepper
- Garlic powder
- Paprika
- Optional: Cumin, oregano, and other spices of your choice

Instructions:

Prepare the Beef:
- Trim excess fat from the beef cuts, leaving a thin layer for flavor.

Curing Process:
- Generously coat the beef with coarse salt, covering all surfaces. Use about 1/4 cup of salt per pound of meat.
- Place the salted beef in a non-reactive container (like glass or plastic) and refrigerate it for about 24 to 48 hours. Turn the meat occasionally to ensure even curing.

Rinsing and Drying:
- After the curing period, rinse the beef thoroughly to remove excess salt. Pat it dry with paper towels.

Seasoning:
- In a bowl, mix black pepper, garlic powder, paprika, and any optional spices you prefer. Adjust the amounts according to your taste.
- Rub the seasoning mixture all over the beef, ensuring it is evenly coated.

Drying:
- Hang the seasoned beef in a well-ventilated area with good airflow or use a food dehydrator. Ensure it is protected from insects and contaminants.
- Allow the beef to air-dry for at least 24 to 48 hours, or until it reaches the desired texture. In a dehydrator, follow the manufacturer's instructions.

Cooking:
- Carne de Sol can be cooked in various ways. One common method is to slice it thinly and grill or fry until it's cooked to your liking.

Serve:
- Carne de Sol is often served with sides like cassava (yuca), rice, beans, and traditional Brazilian accompaniments.

Note: The curing and drying process is essential for developing the unique texture and flavor of Carne de Sol. Adjust the curing and drying times based on your preferences and the thickness of the meat. The finished product should have a firm texture, similar to jerky, with a concentrated beef flavor.

Cuscuz Paulista

Ingredients:

- 2 cups fine couscous
- 1 1/2 cups chicken or vegetable broth
- 2 tablespoons olive oil
- 1 onion, finely chopped
- 2 cloves garlic, minced
- 1 bell pepper, diced
- 1 tomato, diced
- 1/2 cup green peas (fresh or frozen)
- 1/2 cup corn kernels (fresh or frozen)
- 1/2 cup cooked ham or sausage, diced
- 3 boiled eggs, sliced
- Salt and pepper to taste
- Parsley or green onions for garnish (optional)

Instructions:

Prepare Couscous:
- In a mixing bowl, combine the couscous with hot chicken or vegetable broth. Cover and let it sit for about 5 minutes, allowing the couscous to absorb the liquid.

Sauté Vegetables:
- In a large pan, heat olive oil over medium heat. Add the chopped onion and minced garlic. Sauté until the onions are translucent.
- Add the diced bell pepper, tomato, green peas, corn, and the cooked ham or sausage. Cook until the vegetables are tender.

Combine Ingredients:
- Fluff the soaked couscous with a fork to separate the grains. Add the couscous to the pan with the sautéed vegetables and meat. Mix well to combine.

Season:
- Season the mixture with salt and pepper to taste. Adjust the seasoning according to your preference.

Assemble and Steam:
- Line a cuscuz mold or a heatproof dish with slices of boiled eggs.

- Carefully spoon the couscous mixture into the mold, pressing it down gently with the back of the spoon.
- Cover the mold with a lid or aluminum foil and steam the cuscuz for about 20-30 minutes, or until it's set.

Serve:
- Once cooked, carefully invert the cuscuz onto a serving platter.
- Garnish with chopped parsley or green onions if desired.

Cuscuz Paulista is a versatile dish, and the ingredients can be adjusted based on personal preferences. It's often served as a side dish or as a main course for lunch or dinner. Enjoy your Cuscuz Paulista!

Arroz de Carreteiro

Ingredients:

- 2 cups white rice
- 1 lb beef (such as sirloin or flank steak), diced
- 1/2 lb smoked sausage (linguiça calabresa or similar), sliced
- 1 large onion, chopped
- 3 cloves garlic, minced
- 2 tomatoes, diced
- 1 bell pepper, diced
- 2 tablespoons vegetable oil
- 4 cups beef broth
- 1 bay leaf
- Salt and pepper to taste
- Chopped fresh parsley for garnish (optional)

Instructions:

Prepare Ingredients:
- Rinse the rice under cold water and set it aside.
- In a large skillet or pan, heat vegetable oil over medium heat.

Sauté Meat:
- Add diced beef to the skillet and brown it on all sides. Remove the browned beef from the skillet and set it aside.
- In the same skillet, add the sliced smoked sausage and cook until it releases its flavors and gets slightly browned. Remove the sausage and set it aside.

Sauté Vegetables:
- In the same skillet, add chopped onion and minced garlic. Sauté until the onion becomes translucent.
- Add diced tomatoes and bell pepper. Cook until the vegetables soften.

Add Rice:
- Stir in the rinsed rice, ensuring it is well-coated with the flavors in the skillet.

Combine Meat and Sausage:
- Return the browned beef and sausage to the skillet. Mix well with the rice and vegetables.

Pour Beef Broth:
- Pour in the beef broth and add the bay leaf. Season with salt and pepper to taste. Stir to combine all ingredients.

Cook Rice:
- Bring the mixture to a boil, then reduce the heat to low. Cover the skillet with a lid and let it simmer until the rice is cooked and the liquid is absorbed. This usually takes about 15-20 minutes.

Garnish and Serve:
- Once the rice is cooked, fluff it with a fork. Remove the bay leaf.
- Garnish with chopped fresh parsley if desired.

Arroz de Carreteiro is a delicious and hearty one-pot dish, perfect for gatherings and family meals. Serve it hot and enjoy the rich flavors of Brazilian cuisine!

Pacu Assado

Ingredients:

- 1 whole pacu fish (cleaned and scaled)
- Salt and pepper to taste
- Lemon or lime wedges
- Olive oil
- Fresh herbs (such as parsley or cilantro) for garnish
- Optional: Garlic, paprika, or other seasonings of your choice

Instructions:

Prepare the Pacu:
- Ensure the pacu fish is properly cleaned and scaled. Make shallow diagonal cuts on both sides of the fish to help the seasonings penetrate.

Season the Fish:
- Rub the pacu fish with salt, pepper, and any optional seasonings you prefer. You can use a mixture of crushed garlic, paprika, or other herbs and spices.

Marinate:
- Drizzle olive oil over the fish and rub it to coat the skin. Squeeze lemon or lime juice over the fish for added flavor.
- Allow the pacu to marinate for at least 30 minutes to let the flavors meld.

Preheat the Grill or Oven:
- If using a grill, preheat it to medium-high heat. If using an oven, preheat it to 375°F (190°C).

Grill or Roast:
- Place the marinated pacu fish on the grill grates or in a roasting pan if using the oven.
- Cook the fish for about 20-30 minutes or until it's cooked through. Cooking time may vary depending on the size of the fish and the cooking method.
- If grilling, you can turn the fish halfway through the cooking process to ensure even cooking and a crispy skin.

Serve:
- Once the pacu is cooked, transfer it to a serving platter.
- Garnish with fresh herbs and lemon or lime wedges.

Pacu assado is often served with sides like rice, farofa (toasted cassava flour), and a fresh salad. Enjoy the delicious flavors of this Brazilian grilled or roasted fish!

Xinxim de Galinha

Ingredients:

- 2 pounds chicken, cut into pieces
- 1/2 cup lime or lemon juice
- Salt and pepper to taste
- 1/2 cup vegetable oil
- 1 large onion, finely chopped
- 3 cloves garlic, minced
- 1 red bell pepper, chopped
- 1 green bell pepper, chopped
- 1 cup chicken broth
- 1 cup crushed peanuts (unsalted)
- 1/2 cup coconut milk
- 2 tablespoons palm oil (dendê)
- 1 tablespoon tomato paste
- 1 tablespoon ground ginger
- 1 tablespoon ground cumin
- 1 tablespoon ground coriander
- 1 tablespoon chili paste or hot sauce (adjust to taste)
- Chopped cilantro for garnish
- Cooked white rice for serving

Instructions:

Marinate the Chicken:
- In a bowl, marinate the chicken pieces with lime or lemon juice, salt, and pepper. Let it marinate for at least 30 minutes.

Sauté Chicken:
- In a large pot or Dutch oven, heat vegetable oil over medium-high heat. Sauté the marinated chicken until browned on all sides. Remove the chicken and set it aside.

Prepare Aromatics:
- In the same pot, add chopped onions and minced garlic. Sauté until the onions are translucent.

Add Peppers and Spices:
- Add chopped red and green bell peppers to the pot. Cook until the peppers are softened.

- Stir in ground ginger, ground cumin, ground coriander, and chili paste or hot sauce. Cook for a few minutes until the spices are fragrant.

Return Chicken to Pot:
- Return the sautéed chicken to the pot.

Pour Broth and Add Other Ingredients:
- Pour in the chicken broth, crushed peanuts, coconut milk, palm oil, and tomato paste. Mix well to combine all the ingredients.

Simmer:
- Bring the mixture to a boil, then reduce the heat to low. Cover the pot and let it simmer for about 30-40 minutes, or until the chicken is fully cooked and tender.

Adjust Seasoning:
- Adjust the seasoning with salt, pepper, and additional hot sauce if needed.

Serve:
- Serve Xinxim de Galinha over cooked white rice.
- Garnish with chopped cilantro before serving.

Xinxim de Galinha is a rich and flavorful dish that showcases the diverse and vibrant flavors of Brazilian cuisine. Enjoy this delicious chicken stew with its unique combination of ingredients!

Buchada de Bode

Ingredients:

For the Stuffing:

- 2 pounds goat meat, diced
- 1 cup goat liver, diced
- 1 cup goat heart, diced
- 1 cup goat lungs, diced (optional)
- 1 cup cooked rice
- 1 cup chopped fresh parsley
- 1 cup chopped green onions
- 2 tomatoes, diced
- 2 onions, finely chopped
- 4 cloves garlic, minced
- 1 cup goat blood (optional)
- Salt and pepper to taste
- Crushed red pepper flakes (optional, for heat)
- 1/2 cup olive oil

For the Stomach:

- 1 cleaned and prepared goat stomach (tripe)
- 1 cup white vinegar (for cleaning)

Instructions:

Prepare the Goat Stomach:
- Clean the goat stomach thoroughly. Rinse it under cold water and soak it in a solution of water and white vinegar for at least 2 hours to remove any residual odor.

Prepare the Stuffing:
- In a large bowl, combine diced goat meat, liver, heart, and lungs (if using).
- Add cooked rice, chopped parsley, green onions, tomatoes, onions, and minced garlic to the bowl.
- If using goat blood for authenticity, mix it in with the ingredients. Adjust the quantity based on your preference.

- Season the mixture with salt, pepper, and crushed red pepper flakes (if using) to taste.
- Add olive oil and mix all the ingredients thoroughly.

Stuff the Goat Stomach:
- Stuff the cleaned goat stomach with the prepared mixture. Be careful not to overfill, leaving some space for the rice to expand during cooking.

Sew or Tie the Stomach:
- Sew or tie the opening of the stomach to secure the stuffing inside.

Cook:
- Place the stuffed stomach in a large pot and add enough water to cover it.
- Bring the water to a boil and then reduce the heat to simmer. Cook for approximately 2-3 hours or until the stomach is tender.

Serve:
- Once cooked, remove the Buchada de Bode from the pot and let it rest for a few minutes before slicing.

Serve:
- Serve Buchada de Bode slices on a platter, and it's often accompanied by side dishes like rice, beans, and greens.

Buchada de Bode is a dish with strong flavors and cultural significance in certain regions of Brazil. Enjoy it as a unique and traditional culinary experience.

Rabada

Ingredients:

- 2 to 3 pounds oxtail, cut into pieces
- Salt and pepper to taste
- 2 tablespoons vegetable oil
- 1 large onion, chopped
- 3 cloves garlic, minced
- 2 tomatoes, diced
- 2 carrots, sliced
- 2 potatoes, diced
- 1 bay leaf
- 4 cups beef or vegetable broth
- 1 cup red wine (optional)
- Fresh parsley for garnish

Instructions:

Prepare Oxtail:
- Rinse the oxtail pieces under cold water and pat them dry with paper towels. Season the oxtail with salt and pepper.

Sear Oxtail:
- In a large pot or Dutch oven, heat vegetable oil over medium-high heat. Sear the oxtail pieces until browned on all sides. This step enhances the flavor of the broth.

Sauté Aromatics:
- Add chopped onions and minced garlic to the pot. Sauté until the onions are translucent.

Add Vegetables:
- Stir in diced tomatoes, sliced carrots, and diced potatoes. Cook for a few minutes to soften the vegetables.

Pour Broth and Wine:
- Pour in the beef or vegetable broth and red wine (if using). Add a bay leaf for extra flavor.

Simmer:

- Bring the mixture to a boil, then reduce the heat to low. Cover the pot and let it simmer for about 2 to 3 hours, or until the oxtail is tender. Stir occasionally.

Check Seasoning:
- Taste the broth and adjust the seasoning with salt and pepper as needed.

Serve:
- Once the oxtail is tender and the flavors have melded, remove the bay leaf.
- Serve Rabada hot, garnished with fresh parsley.

Rabada is often enjoyed with rice or crusty bread to soak up the flavorful broth. It's a comforting and hearty dish, popular in Brazilian cuisine for its delicious taste and the richness of oxtail.

Sarapatel

Ingredients:

- 1.5 to 2 pounds pork offal (heart, liver, lungs), cleaned and diced
- 1 cup white vinegar (for cleaning)
- 2 cups white wine or water
- 2 tablespoons vegetable oil
- 1 large onion, finely chopped
- 4 cloves garlic, minced
- 2 tomatoes, diced
- 2 bay leaves
- 1 teaspoon ground cumin
- 1 teaspoon paprika
- Salt and pepper to taste
- 1 cup tomato sauce
- 2 cups pork or beef broth
- 1 cup cooked blood (optional)
- Chopped fresh parsley for garnish
- Cooked rice for serving

Instructions:

Clean the Offal:
- Clean the pork offal thoroughly under cold running water. Soak the offal in a solution of white vinegar and water for about 30 minutes to remove any strong odors.

Cook the Offal:
- In a large pot, combine the cleaned and diced offal with white wine or water. Bring to a boil, then reduce the heat to simmer. Cook for about 30-40 minutes until the offal is tender. Drain and set aside.

Sauté Aromatics:
- In a separate pot, heat vegetable oil over medium heat. Add chopped onions and minced garlic. Sauté until the onions are translucent.

Add Tomatoes and Spices:
- Add diced tomatoes, bay leaves, ground cumin, paprika, salt, and pepper. Cook until the tomatoes break down and the spices are fragrant.

Incorporate Offal:

- Add the cooked and drained offal to the pot. Mix well with the aromatics and spices.

Pour Tomato Sauce and Broth:
- Pour in tomato sauce and pork or beef broth. Stir to combine all the ingredients.

Simmer:
- Bring the mixture to a simmer and let it cook for about 20-30 minutes, allowing the flavors to meld.

Optional: Add Blood (if using):
- If using cooked blood for authenticity, stir it into the pot and cook for an additional 10 minutes. Adjust the seasoning if needed.

Serve:
- Remove the bay leaves and discard them.
- Serve Sarapatel hot over cooked rice, garnished with chopped fresh parsley.

Sarapatel is a dish with robust flavors and cultural significance in certain regions of Brazil. Enjoy it as a unique and traditional culinary experience.

Beijinho

Ingredients:

- 1 can (14 ounces) sweetened condensed milk
- 2 tablespoons unsweetened shredded coconut, plus extra for rolling
- 1 tablespoon unsalted butter
- Butter or oil (for greasing hands)

Instructions:

Prepare the Mixture:
- In a non-stick pan, combine the sweetened condensed milk, shredded coconut, and butter.

Cook the Mixture:
- Cook the mixture over medium heat, stirring continuously to avoid sticking to the bottom of the pan.
- Continue cooking until the mixture thickens and starts to pull away from the sides of the pan. It should have a consistency similar to soft fudge.

Cool the Mixture:
- Remove the pan from heat and let the mixture cool for a few minutes. It should be cool enough to handle.

Shape into Balls:
- Grease your hands with a bit of butter or oil to prevent sticking. Take small portions of the mixture and roll them into bite-sized balls between your palms.

Coat with Coconut:
- Roll each beijinho ball in additional shredded coconut, ensuring an even coating.

Serve:
- Place the beijinhos on a plate or tray.
- You can insert a small piece of clove into the top of each beijinho for decoration (optional).

Chill (Optional):
- You can let the beijinhos chill in the refrigerator for a couple of hours to firm up, but they can also be enjoyed at room temperature.

Serve and Enjoy:
- Beijinhos are ready to be served. Enjoy these delightful coconut treats!

Beijinho is a favorite Brazilian sweet, and its name translates to "little kiss." It's a simple yet delicious dessert that is sure to be a hit at any gathering.

Cuscuz Branco

Ingredients:

- 1 cup tapioca or manioc starch
- 4 cups whole milk
- 1 cup sugar
- 1 cup coconut milk
- 1/2 cup shredded coconut (optional)
- Pinch of salt
- Cinnamon for garnish (optional)

Instructions:

Prepare the Tapioca Starch:
- In a bowl, combine the tapioca or manioc starch with 2 cups of whole milk. Mix well to form a smooth paste.

Heat Milk and Sugar:
- In a saucepan, heat the remaining 2 cups of whole milk over medium heat. Add sugar and a pinch of salt. Stir until the sugar is completely dissolved.

Add Tapioca Mixture:
- Once the milk is heated, slowly add the tapioca mixture while stirring continuously to avoid lumps.

Cook the Mixture:
- Continue cooking the mixture over medium heat, stirring constantly. The mixture will start to thicken.

Add Coconut Milk:
- When the mixture reaches a custard-like consistency, add coconut milk. Keep stirring until the mixture becomes thick and creamy.

Optional: Add Shredded Coconut:
- If you like, add shredded coconut to the mixture and stir well. This adds texture and extra coconut flavor.

Simmer:
- Reduce the heat to low and let the cuscuz branco simmer for a few more minutes, ensuring it's well-cooked and has a pudding-like consistency.

Cool and Serve:
- Remove the cuscuz branco from heat and let it cool slightly.

- Transfer the mixture to serving dishes or molds. Allow it to cool completely before refrigerating.

Chill (Optional):
- For a firmer texture, refrigerate the cuscuz branco for a few hours or overnight.

Serve and Garnish:
- Serve chilled or at room temperature. Optionally, sprinkle cinnamon on top for added flavor and decoration.

Cuscuz Branco is a delightful and comforting Brazilian dessert with a creamy and slightly chewy texture. It's perfect for satisfying a sweet tooth and is often enjoyed on various occasions.

Linguiça Mineira

Ingredients:

- 2 pounds pork shoulder, coarsely ground
- 1/2 pound pork fatback, coarsely ground
- 3 tablespoons sweet paprika
- 2 tablespoons garlic powder
- 2 tablespoons onion powder
- 1 tablespoon cumin
- 1 tablespoon coriander
- 1 tablespoon black pepper, freshly ground
- 1 tablespoon smoked paprika (optional, for a smoky flavor)
- 2 teaspoons salt
- Natural hog casings, soaked in water (if making links)

Instructions:

Prepare the Meat:
- Coarsely grind the pork shoulder and pork fatback using a meat grinder.

Mix the Spices:
- In a large mixing bowl, combine sweet paprika, garlic powder, onion powder, cumin, coriander, black pepper, smoked paprika (if using), and salt. Mix well to create a spice blend.

Season the Meat:
- Add the spice blend to the ground pork and fatback. Mix thoroughly to ensure even distribution of spices throughout the meat.

Refrigerate:
- Cover the seasoned meat and let it marinate in the refrigerator for at least a few hours or overnight. This allows the flavors to meld.

Stuff the Sausage (Optional):
- If making links, soak natural hog casings in water according to the package instructions. Stuff the casings with the seasoned meat using a sausage stuffer or a funnel attachment on your meat grinder.

Shape the Sausage:
- Twist the sausage mixture into individual links, or leave it as a long coil if you prefer.

Air-Dry (Optional):

- If making links, you can let the sausages air-dry for an hour or so. This step helps the casings dry and gives the sausages a firmer texture.

Cook:
- Grill, pan-fry, or bake the Linguiça Mineira until fully cooked. The internal temperature should reach at least 160°F (71°C).

Serve:
- Once cooked, serve the Linguiça Mineira hot. It can be enjoyed on its own, as part of a sandwich, or as a flavorful addition to various dishes.

Linguiça Mineira is appreciated for its robust flavors, and it can be a versatile ingredient in different recipes. Adjust the spice levels according to your taste preferences.

Tutu de Feijão

Ingredients:

- 2 cups cooked black beans (with some of the cooking liquid reserved)
- 1 cup cassava flour (farinha de mandioca)
- 2 tablespoons vegetable oil or lard
- 1 onion, finely chopped
- 3 cloves garlic, minced
- 1 bay leaf
- Salt and pepper to taste
- 1/2 cup chopped parsley or green onions (for garnish)

Instructions:

Prepare the Black Beans:
- Cook the black beans until they are soft. You can use canned beans or cook them from dry according to the package instructions. Reserve some of the cooking liquid.

Mash the Beans:
- In a large pot, mash the cooked black beans using a potato masher or the back of a spoon. Add some of the reserved cooking liquid to achieve a creamy consistency. The amount of liquid depends on your preference.

Sauté Onions and Garlic:
- In a separate pan, heat vegetable oil or lard over medium heat. Add finely chopped onions and minced garlic. Sauté until the onions are translucent.

Add Cassava Flour:
- Add cassava flour (farinha de mandioca) to the sautéed onions and garlic. Stir well to combine and let it cook for a few minutes.

Combine with Mashed Beans:
- Add the sautéed cassava flour mixture to the mashed black beans. Stir well to combine, ensuring a smooth and creamy texture. If needed, add more cooking liquid to reach your desired consistency.

Season:
- Season the Tutu de Feijão with salt, pepper, and add a bay leaf for extra flavor. Stir well.

Simmer:

- Let the Tutu de Feijão simmer on low heat for about 15-20 minutes, stirring occasionally to prevent sticking.

Garnish:
- Before serving, garnish with chopped parsley or green onions for freshness and color.

Serve:
- Tutu de Feijão is ready to be served. It can be served as a side dish with rice, as part of a feijoada, or alongside grilled meats.

Enjoy this traditional Brazilian dish that showcases the rich flavors of black beans and cassava flour!

Manjar Branco

Ingredients:

- 1 cup cornstarch
- 4 cups coconut milk
- 1 cup sugar
- 1 teaspoon vanilla extract
- Coconut flakes for garnish (optional)
- Fruit sauce or caramel sauce for serving (optional)

Instructions:

Dissolve Cornstarch:
- In a bowl, dissolve cornstarch in a small amount of coconut milk, ensuring there are no lumps.

Heat Coconut Milk and Sugar:
- In a saucepan, combine the remaining coconut milk and sugar. Heat the mixture over medium heat, stirring constantly until the sugar is completely dissolved.

Add Cornstarch Mixture:
- Pour the dissolved cornstarch into the saucepan with the coconut milk and sugar. Continue stirring to combine.

Cook the Mixture:
- Cook the mixture over medium heat, stirring continuously to prevent lumps. Continue cooking until the mixture thickens and reaches a pudding-like consistency.

Add Vanilla:
- Once the mixture has thickened, remove it from heat and stir in the vanilla extract. Mix well to incorporate the vanilla flavor.

Pour into Molds:
- Pour the manjar branco mixture into individual molds or a large serving mold. Allow it to cool slightly before placing it in the refrigerator.

Chill:
- Refrigerate the manjar branco for at least 3-4 hours or until it is completely set.

Serve:
- Once set, unmold the manjar branco onto a serving platter.
- Garnish with coconut flakes if desired.

Optional Sauce:
- Serve the manjar branco on its own or drizzle with fruit sauce (such as passion fruit or raspberry) or caramel sauce.

Slice and Enjoy:
- Slice the manjar branco into portions and serve chilled.

Manjar Branco is a delightful and refreshing dessert that is perfect for warm days or as a sweet ending to a Brazilian meal. It's enjoyed for its smooth and creamy texture with a subtle coconut flavor.

Cocada

Ingredients:

- 3 cups shredded coconut (fresh or desiccated)
- 2 cups granulated sugar
- 1 cup water
- 1/2 teaspoon vanilla extract (optional)
- Pinch of salt

Instructions:

Prepare the Coconut:
- If using fresh coconut, grate or shred it. If using desiccated coconut, measure out 3 cups.

Combine Sugar and Water:
- In a large saucepan, combine the granulated sugar and water. Place it over medium heat.

Make Sugar Syrup:
- Stir the sugar and water mixture until the sugar dissolves. Allow it to come to a simmer.

Add Shredded Coconut:
- Once the sugar has dissolved and the mixture is simmering, add the shredded coconut to the saucepan.

Cook the Cocada:
- Cook the mixture over medium heat, stirring continuously to prevent sticking. The goal is to evaporate most of the water and achieve a thick, sticky consistency.

Add Vanilla Extract (Optional):
- If using vanilla extract, add it to the mixture and stir well.

Continue Cooking:
- Keep cooking and stirring until the coconut-sugar mixture reaches a consistency where you can see the bottom of the pan for a moment when you drag the spoon through the mixture.

Check for Doneness:
- To check if it's done, take a small amount and let it cool on a plate. It should become firm and hold its shape.

Remove from Heat:

- Once the desired consistency is reached, remove the saucepan from the heat.

Cool and Serve:
- Allow the cocada mixture to cool for a few minutes. It will continue to firm up as it cools.
- Spoon the cocada into small mounds on a greased or lined tray, or press it into a pan for cutting into squares.

Serve:
- Once completely cool and firm, the cocada is ready to be served. Enjoy this delicious coconut treat!

Cocada can be enjoyed on its own or used as a topping for other desserts. It's a delightful and simple sweet treat that showcases the tropical flavor of coconut.

Pé-de-Moleque

Ingredients:

- 2 cups roasted peanuts (skinless)
- 1 cup rapadura (or jaggery), grated, or brown sugar
- 1 cup granulated sugar
- 1 cup water
- 1 tablespoon unsalted butter
- Pinch of salt

Instructions:

Prepare Roasted Peanuts:
- Roast the peanuts in a pan or oven until they are golden brown. Remove the skins by rubbing the peanuts between your hands or using a clean kitchen towel.

Prepare a Baking Sheet:
- Line a baking sheet with parchment paper or grease it with butter to prevent sticking.

Chop Peanuts:
- Once the peanuts are roasted and skinned, roughly chop them into smaller pieces. You can leave some whole peanuts for texture.

Prepare Rapadura (or Jaggery):
- Grate the rapadura or jaggery. If using brown sugar, measure it out.

Make Sugar Syrup:
- In a saucepan, combine granulated sugar and water over medium heat. Stir until the sugar is completely dissolved.

Cook the Sugar Syrup:
- Allow the sugar syrup to come to a boil, then reduce the heat to medium-low. Cook the syrup until it reaches a soft-ball stage. You can test this by dropping a small amount into cold water – it should form a soft ball that can be flattened when pressed between your fingers.

Add Butter and Salt:
- Once the sugar syrup reaches the desired consistency, add unsalted butter and a pinch of salt. Stir until the butter is melted and incorporated.

Add Peanuts and Rapadura:
- Add the chopped peanuts and grated rapadura (or jaggery) to the sugar syrup. Stir well to coat the peanuts evenly.

Cook Until Golden:
- Continue cooking the mixture over medium heat, stirring continuously, until it turns golden brown and starts to pull away from the sides of the pan.

Transfer to Baking Sheet:
- Quickly transfer the hot pé-de-moleque mixture to the prepared baking sheet, spreading it out evenly.

Flatten and Cool:
- Use a spatula or the back of a spoon to flatten the pé-de-moleque on the baking sheet. Allow it to cool and set completely.

Cut into Pieces:
- Once cooled and firm, cut the pé-de-moleque into squares or rectangles using a sharp knife.

Pé-de-moleque is ready to be enjoyed as a sweet and crunchy snack. It's a popular treat during festivities, especially during traditional celebrations like Festa Junina in Brazil.

Arroz Doce

Ingredients:

- 1 cup white rice
- 4 cups whole milk
- 1 cup granulated sugar
- 1 cinnamon stick
- 1 tablespoon unsalted butter
- 1/2 teaspoon vanilla extract
- Ground cinnamon for garnish

Instructions:

Rinse the Rice:
- Rinse the white rice under cold water until the water runs clear. This helps remove excess starch.

Cook the Rice:
- In a large saucepan, combine the rinsed rice and 2 cups of whole milk. Cook over medium heat, stirring occasionally, until the rice is partially cooked.

Add Sugar and Cinnamon Stick:
- Add granulated sugar and a cinnamon stick to the partially cooked rice. Stir well to combine.

Continue Cooking:
- Continue cooking the rice mixture over medium heat, gradually adding the remaining 2 cups of whole milk. Stir frequently to prevent sticking.

Simmer Until Rice is Tender:
- Simmer the rice mixture until the rice is tender and the mixture becomes creamy. This may take about 20-30 minutes.

Add Butter and Vanilla:
- Once the rice is cooked and the mixture is creamy, stir in unsalted butter and vanilla extract. Mix well to incorporate.

Remove Cinnamon Stick:
- Remove the cinnamon stick from the rice pudding. If you like a stronger cinnamon flavor, you can leave it in, but be sure to inform your guests.

Serve Warm or Chilled:
- Arroz Doce can be served warm or chilled, depending on your preference.

Garnish with Ground Cinnamon:

- Before serving, sprinkle ground cinnamon on top for garnish.

Serve in Bowls:
- Spoon the Arroz Doce into individual bowls or a large serving dish.

Arroz Doce is a comforting and delicious dessert that captures the essence of Brazilian cuisine. Whether enjoyed warm or chilled, it's a delightful treat for various occasions.

Canjiquinha

Ingredients:

- 1 cup canjiquinha (hominy corn)
- 1 tablespoon vegetable oil
- 1 onion, finely chopped
- 3 cloves garlic, minced
- 1 pound smoked sausage, sliced (linguiça or calabresa)
- 1 carrot, diced
- 2 potatoes, diced
- 1 bay leaf
- 8 cups water or chicken broth
- Salt and pepper to taste
- Chopped fresh parsley for garnish

Instructions:

Rinse Canjiquinha:
- Rinse the canjiquinha under cold water and drain.

Sauté Onion and Garlic:
- In a large pot, heat vegetable oil over medium heat. Add finely chopped onion and minced garlic. Sauté until the onions are translucent.

Add Sausage:
- Add sliced smoked sausage to the pot. Cook until the sausage is browned and releases its flavor.

Add Vegetables:
- Stir in diced carrot and potatoes. Cook for a few minutes until the vegetables start to soften.

Add Canjiquinha:
- Add the rinsed canjiquinha to the pot. Mix well with the other ingredients.

Pour Water or Broth:
- Pour in water or chicken broth, ensuring that all the ingredients are submerged. Add a bay leaf for extra flavor.

Season:
- Season the soup with salt and pepper to taste. Stir well.

Simmer:

- Bring the soup to a boil, then reduce the heat to low. Cover the pot and let it simmer for about 1 to 1.5 hours, or until the canjiquinha is tender and the flavors meld.

Adjust Seasoning:
- Taste the soup and adjust the seasoning if needed.

Serve:
- Ladle the canjiquinha soup into bowls.
- Garnish with chopped fresh parsley before serving.

Canjiquinha soup is a comforting and filling dish, perfect for warming up on chilly days. It's a popular choice in Brazilian cuisine, and you can customize it by adding other vegetables or seasonings to suit your taste.

Escondidinho

Ingredients:

For the Cassava Puree:

- 2 pounds cassava (mandioca or aipim), peeled and cut into chunks
- 1 cup milk
- 2 tablespoons butter
- Salt to taste

For the Chicken Filling:

- 1 pound chicken breast, cooked and shredded
- 1 onion, finely chopped
- 2 cloves garlic, minced
- 1 tomato, diced
- 1 cup chicken broth
- 1 tablespoon tomato paste
- 1 teaspoon cumin
- 1 teaspoon paprika
- Salt and pepper to taste
- 2 tablespoons vegetable oil

For Assembling:

- Grated Parmesan cheese (optional, for topping)
- Chopped fresh parsley (for garnish)

Instructions:

Prepare the Cassava Puree:
- Boil the cassava chunks in salted water until they are tender. Drain and mash them while still hot.
- In a separate saucepan, heat the milk and butter. Add the mashed cassava and continue to mash until you achieve a smooth consistency. Season with salt to taste.

Prepare the Chicken Filling:
- In a skillet, heat vegetable oil over medium heat. Add chopped onions and minced garlic. Sauté until the onions are translucent.

- Add shredded chicken to the skillet and cook for a few minutes until it starts to brown.
- Stir in diced tomatoes, tomato paste, cumin, paprika, salt, and pepper. Cook for additional minutes.
- Pour in chicken broth and let the mixture simmer until it thickens and flavors meld.

Assemble Escondidinho:
- Preheat the oven to 350°F (180°C).
- In a baking dish, spread half of the cassava puree as the bottom layer.
- Add the chicken filling on top of the cassava layer.
- Cover the chicken filling with the remaining cassava puree.

Bake:
- If desired, sprinkle grated Parmesan cheese on top.
- Bake in the preheated oven for about 20-25 minutes or until the top is golden and the edges are bubbling.

Serve:
- Remove from the oven and let it cool slightly before serving.
- Garnish with chopped fresh parsley and serve Escondidinho hot.

Escondidinho is a comforting and flavorful dish that combines the creamy texture of mashed cassava with a savory filling. Feel free to customize the filling or toppings based on your preferences.

Frango com Quiabo

Ingredients:

- 1 whole chicken, cut into serving pieces
- 1/4 cup lime or lemon juice
- Salt and pepper to taste
- 2 tablespoons vegetable oil
- 1 onion, finely chopped
- 3 cloves garlic, minced
- 2 tomatoes, diced
- 2 cups fresh okra, trimmed and sliced
- 1 bell pepper, diced
- 1 cup chicken broth
- 1 bay leaf
- 1 teaspoon ground cumin
- 1 teaspoon paprika
- 1/2 teaspoon dried thyme
- Fresh cilantro or parsley for garnish
- Cooked rice for serving

Instructions:

Marinate the Chicken:
- In a bowl, marinate the chicken pieces with lime or lemon juice, salt, and pepper. Let it marinate for at least 30 minutes.

Brown the Chicken:
- In a large pot or Dutch oven, heat vegetable oil over medium-high heat. Brown the marinated chicken pieces on all sides. Remove and set aside.

Sauté Aromatics:
- In the same pot, add chopped onions and minced garlic. Sauté until the onions are translucent.

Add Tomatoes and Spices:
- Stir in diced tomatoes, ground cumin, paprika, and dried thyme. Cook until the tomatoes are softened.

Return Chicken to the Pot:
- Return the browned chicken pieces to the pot, along with any accumulated juices.

Add Vegetables:
- Add sliced okra and diced bell pepper to the pot. Mix well with the chicken and aromatics.

Pour Chicken Broth:
- Pour in chicken broth and add a bay leaf. Bring the mixture to a simmer.

Simmer:
- Reduce the heat to low, cover the pot, and let the Frango com Quiabo simmer for about 30-40 minutes or until the chicken is cooked through and tender.

Check Seasoning:
- Taste the dish and adjust the seasoning with salt and pepper if needed.

Garnish and Serve:
- Garnish with fresh cilantro or parsley.
- Serve Frango com Quiabo over cooked rice.

Frango com Quiabo is a delicious and comforting dish that highlights the unique flavor of okra. The combination of chicken and vegetables makes it a wholesome and satisfying meal.

Quibebe

Ingredients:

- 1 kg butternut squash or pumpkin, peeled and diced
- 1 onion, finely chopped
- 2 tablespoons vegetable oil
- 2 cloves garlic, minced
- 1 cup diced tomatoes
- 1 cup corn kernels (fresh or frozen)
- 1 teaspoon ground cumin
- Salt and pepper to taste
- Fresh cilantro or parsley for garnish

Instructions:

Prepare the Squash:
- Peel and dice the butternut squash or pumpkin into small, uniform-sized pieces.

Sauté Onions and Garlic:
- In a large pot, heat vegetable oil over medium heat. Add finely chopped onions and minced garlic. Sauté until the onions are translucent.

Add Squash:
- Add the diced squash to the pot. Stir well to coat the squash with the sautéed onions and garlic.

Cook Squash:
- Cook the squash for about 5-7 minutes, stirring occasionally.

Add Tomatoes and Corn:
- Add diced tomatoes and corn kernels to the pot. Mix well with the squash.

Season:
- Sprinkle ground cumin over the mixture. Season with salt and pepper to taste. Stir to combine.

Simmer:
- Reduce the heat to low, cover the pot, and let the quibebe simmer until the squash is tender. This may take about 20-30 minutes.

Check Seasoning:
- Taste and adjust the seasoning if needed.

Garnish:
- Garnish with chopped fresh cilantro or parsley before serving.

Serve:

- Quibebe is ready to be served. It can be enjoyed as a side dish or a light vegetarian main course.

Quibebe is a comforting and flavorful dish that highlights the natural sweetness of the squash. It's a popular addition to Brazilian meals, especially during the fall and winter seasons.

Doce de Abóbora

Ingredients:

- 1 kg butternut squash or pumpkin, peeled and diced
- 2 cups sugar
- 1 cinnamon stick
- 3 cloves
- 1 cup water
- Grated coconut for garnish (optional)

Instructions:

Prepare the Squash:
- Peel and remove the seeds from the butternut squash or pumpkin. Cut it into small, uniform-sized cubes.

Cook the Squash:
- In a large pot, combine the diced squash, sugar, cinnamon stick, cloves, and water.

Simmer:
- Bring the mixture to a boil, then reduce the heat to low. Let it simmer gently, stirring occasionally, until the squash is tender and the syrup has thickened. This may take about 30-40 minutes.

Check Consistency:
- Test the consistency of the syrup by placing a small amount on a cold plate. It should set and form a jelly-like consistency.

Remove Spices:
- Once the squash is cooked and the syrup is the right consistency, remove the cinnamon stick and cloves.

Cool:
- Allow the Doce de Abóbora to cool to room temperature.

Serve:
- Serve the Doce de Abóbora in small bowls or plates.

Garnish (Optional):
- Optionally, garnish with grated coconut on top.

Enjoy:
- Enjoy this sweet and spiced pumpkin dessert, a popular treat in Brazilian households.

Feel free to adjust the sugar quantity based on your sweetness preference. This dessert is a delightful way to showcase the natural flavors of pumpkin with a hint of warm spices.

Arroz Carreteiro

Ingredients:

- 2 cups white rice
- 500g beef chuck or sirloin, diced
- 1 onion, finely chopped
- 3 cloves garlic, minced
- 2 tomatoes, diced
- 1 bell pepper, diced
- 2 tablespoons vegetable oil
- 1 teaspoon cumin
- 1 teaspoon paprika
- Salt and pepper to taste
- Fresh parsley for garnish

Instructions:

Cook the Rice:
- Rinse the rice under cold water until the water runs clear. Cook the rice according to package instructions.

Sauté Beef:
- In a large skillet or pan, heat vegetable oil over medium-high heat. Add diced beef and cook until browned on all sides.

Add Aromatics:
- Add chopped onions and minced garlic to the skillet. Sauté until the onions are translucent.

Stir in Vegetables:
- Stir in diced tomatoes and bell pepper. Cook until the vegetables are softened.

Season:
- Sprinkle cumin, paprika, salt, and pepper over the beef and vegetables. Mix well to coat everything evenly.

Combine with Rice:
- Add the cooked rice to the skillet with the beef and vegetables. Mix thoroughly, ensuring the rice is well-coated with the flavors.

Simmer:
- Let the Arroz Carreteiro simmer for a few minutes, allowing the flavors to meld.

Check Seasoning:

- Taste and adjust the seasoning if needed.

Garnish:
- Garnish with freshly chopped parsley before serving.

Serve:
- Arroz Carreteiro is ready to be served. It can be enjoyed on its own or paired with a simple salad.

Arroz Carreteiro is a hearty and flavorful dish that originated from the Brazilian gauchos or cowboys. It's a comforting meal that combines rice with tender beef and aromatic spices.

Virado à Paulista

Ingredients:

- 2 cups black beans, cooked
- 300g pork shoulder, diced
- 200g bacon, chopped
- 1 smoked sausage (linguiça), sliced
- 1 onion, finely chopped
- 3 cloves garlic, minced
- 2 cups collard greens, finely sliced
- 3 eggs, fried
- 2 bananas, sliced and fried (optional)
- 2 cups rice, cooked
- 2 tablespoons vegetable oil
- Salt and pepper to taste

Instructions:

Prepare the Beans:
- Cook the black beans until tender. If using canned beans, drain and rinse them.

Sauté Pork and Bacon:
- In a large pan, heat vegetable oil over medium-high heat. Add diced pork shoulder and chopped bacon. Cook until browned.

Add Sausage and Aromatics:
- Stir in sliced smoked sausage and cook until it releases its flavors. Add chopped onions and minced garlic. Sauté until the onions are translucent.

Combine with Beans:
- Add the cooked black beans to the pan. Mix well and let it simmer for a few minutes to allow flavors to meld.

Prepare Collard Greens:
- In a separate pan, sauté finely sliced collard greens until wilted. Season with salt and pepper.

Fry Eggs:
- Fry eggs in a separate pan, keeping the yolks runny.

Assemble the Dish:
- Serve the Virado à Paulista by arranging the following on a plate: a portion of beans, collard greens, rice, fried eggs, and fried bananas (if using).

Season:

- Season the dish with salt and pepper to taste.

Serve:
- Virado à Paulista is traditionally served hot. Ensure each element is well placed on the plate.

Enjoy:
- Enjoy this classic São Paulo-style dish, a rich and hearty combination of beans, meats, greens, and rice.

Virado à Paulista is a flavorful and satisfying dish that reflects the culinary traditions of São Paulo. The combination of beans, meats, and accompaniments creates a well-balanced and delicious meal.

Bolinho de Bacalhau

Ingredients:

- 500g salted codfish (bacalhau), soaked and desalted
- 4 cups potatoes, peeled and diced
- 1 onion, finely chopped
- 2 cloves garlic, minced
- 1/4 cup fresh parsley, finely chopped
- 2 eggs, beaten
- Salt and black pepper to taste
- Vegetable oil for frying
- Lemon wedges for serving

Instructions:

- Prepare the Codfish:
    - Soak the salted codfish in water for at least 24 hours, changing the water several times to remove excess salt. After soaking, shred the codfish into small pieces.
- Boil Potatoes:
    - Boil the peeled and diced potatoes until they are soft and can be easily mashed.
- Mash Potatoes:
    - Mash the boiled potatoes thoroughly.
- Sauté Onions and Garlic:
    - In a pan, sauté finely chopped onions and minced garlic until they are soft and golden.
- Combine Ingredients:
    - In a large bowl, mix the shredded codfish, mashed potatoes, sautéed onions and garlic, chopped parsley, beaten eggs, salt, and black pepper. Combine the ingredients well.
- Form Balls:
    - With moistened hands, take portions of the mixture and form small balls, about the size of a walnut.
- Fry the Bolinhos:
    - Heat vegetable oil in a deep fryer or a heavy-bottomed pan. Fry the codfish balls until they are golden brown and crispy.
- Drain Excess Oil:
    - Place the fried bolinhos on paper towels to drain excess oil.

Serve:
- Serve the Bolinho de Bacalhau hot, accompanied by lemon wedges for squeezing over the top.

Enjoy:
- Enjoy these delightful codfish balls as a tasty appetizer or snack.

Bolinho de Bacalhau is a popular Brazilian dish, especially during festive occasions. The combination of salted codfish with potatoes and aromatic herbs creates a flavorful and crispy treat.

Arroz de Forno

Ingredients:

- 2 cups white rice
- 4 cups chicken or vegetable broth
- 1 onion, finely chopped
- 2 cloves garlic, minced
- 1 bell pepper, diced
- 1 cup frozen peas
- 1 cup corn kernels (fresh or frozen)
- 1/2 cup tomato sauce
- 1/4 cup olive oil
- 1 teaspoon paprika
- Salt and pepper to taste
- Fresh parsley for garnish

Instructions:

Preheat Oven:
- Preheat your oven to 350°F (180°C).

Prepare Rice:
- Rinse the white rice under cold water until the water runs clear. In a large oven-safe dish, combine the rice and broth.

Sauté Aromatics:
- In a pan, heat olive oil over medium heat. Add chopped onions and minced garlic. Sauté until the onions are translucent.

Add Vegetables:
- Stir in diced bell pepper, frozen peas, and corn kernels. Cook for a few minutes until the vegetables are slightly tender.

Combine with Rice:
- Add the sautéed vegetables to the rice and broth mixture in the oven-safe dish. Mix well.

Season:
- Season the mixture with paprika, salt, and pepper. Add tomato sauce and stir until everything is evenly distributed.

Cover and Bake:
- Cover the dish with a lid or aluminum foil. Bake in the preheated oven for about 25-30 minutes or until the rice is cooked and the liquid is absorbed.

Check Doneness:

- Check the rice for doneness. If needed, you can bake for an additional 5-10 minutes.

Garnish:
- Garnish the Arroz de Forno with fresh parsley before serving.

Serve:
- Serve this baked rice as a delicious side dish or a standalone meal.

Arroz de Forno is a comforting and flavorful baked rice dish that incorporates a variety of vegetables. It's a versatile recipe that can be customized with your favorite veggies and herbs.

Ensopado de Borrego

Ingredients:

- 1.5 kg lamb shoulder, cut into cubes
- 2 tablespoons olive oil
- 1 large onion, finely chopped
- 4 cloves garlic, minced
- 2 tomatoes, diced
- 1 bell pepper, diced
- 2 carrots, sliced
- 1 cup peas (fresh or frozen)
- 1 cup white wine
- 4 cups beef or lamb broth
- 2 bay leaves
- 1 teaspoon dried thyme
- 1 teaspoon paprika
- Salt and black pepper to taste
- Fresh parsley for garnish

Instructions:

Sear the Lamb:
- In a large pot, heat olive oil over medium-high heat. Sear the lamb cubes until browned on all sides. Remove lamb and set aside.

Sauté Aromatics:
- In the same pot, add chopped onions and minced garlic. Sauté until the onions are translucent.

Add Vegetables:
- Stir in diced tomatoes, bell pepper, carrots, and peas. Cook for a few minutes until the vegetables start to soften.

Deglaze with Wine:
- Pour white wine into the pot, scraping the bottom to deglaze and pick up any flavorful bits. Allow it to simmer for a couple of minutes.

Return Lamb to the Pot:
- Return the seared lamb cubes to the pot.

Pour Broth:
- Add beef or lamb broth to the pot. Ensure that the meat is covered with liquid.

Season:

- Add bay leaves, dried thyme, paprika, salt, and black pepper. Stir to combine.

Simmer:
- Reduce the heat to low, cover the pot, and let the stew simmer for 1.5 to 2 hours or until the lamb is tender.

Check Seasoning:
- Taste and adjust the seasoning if necessary.

Garnish and Serve:
- Garnish with fresh parsley before serving. Serve Ensopado de Borrego hot with crusty bread or over rice.

Ensopado de Borrego is a comforting and hearty lamb stew with a rich blend of vegetables and aromatic herbs. It's a perfect dish for colder days or special occasions.

Mocotó

Ingredients:

- 1.5 kg lamb, cut into stew pieces
- 2 tablespoons olive oil
- 1 large onion, chopped
- 3 cloves garlic, minced
- 2 tomatoes, diced
- 1 bell pepper, diced
- 2 carrots, sliced
- 2 potatoes, diced
- 1 cup peas (fresh or frozen)
- 1 cup red wine
- 4 cups beef or lamb broth
- 2 bay leaves
- 1 teaspoon dried thyme
- Salt and pepper to taste
- Fresh parsley for garnish

Instructions:

In a large pot, heat olive oil over medium heat. Brown the lamb pieces on all sides.
Add chopped onions and minced garlic, sauté until onions are translucent.
Pour in red wine and let it simmer for a couple of minutes.
Add diced tomatoes, bell pepper, carrots, and potatoes to the pot.
Pour in beef or lamb broth, add bay leaves, dried thyme, salt, and pepper.
Bring the stew to a boil, then reduce the heat to low, cover, and let it simmer for 1.5 to 2 hours or until the lamb is tender.
In the last 15 minutes of cooking, add peas.
Adjust the seasoning if needed and garnish with fresh parsley before serving.

Mocotó:

Mocotó is a Brazilian dish made from cow's feet. The following is a basic recipe for Mocotó:

Ingredients:

- 2 cow's feet, cleaned and split
- Water for boiling

- 1 onion, chopped
- 3 cloves garlic, minced
- 2 tomatoes, diced
- 1 bell pepper, diced
- 1 cup cooked white beans
- 1 cup beef broth
- 1 bay leaf
- 1 teaspoon ground cumin
- Salt and pepper to taste
- Fresh cilantro for garnish

Instructions:

Clean and split the cow's feet, then boil them in water until they become tender.
In a separate pot, sauté chopped onions and minced garlic until golden.
Add diced tomatoes, bell pepper, and cooked white beans to the pot.
Pour in beef broth, add bay leaf, ground cumin, salt, and pepper.
Once the cow's feet are tender, transfer them to the pot with the other ingredients.
Simmer the Mocotó for an additional 20-30 minutes.
Adjust the seasoning if needed and garnish with fresh cilantro before serving.

Both Ensopado de Borrego and Mocotó are hearty and flavorful Brazilian dishes that showcase the richness of Brazilian cuisine.

Frango à Passarinho

Ingredients:

- 1.5 kg lamb meat, cut into chunks
- 2 tablespoons vegetable oil
- 1 onion, finely chopped
- 3 cloves garlic, minced
- 2 tomatoes, diced
- 1 cup red wine
- 4 cups beef or lamb broth
- 3 carrots, sliced
- 3 potatoes, diced
- 1 cup green peas (fresh or frozen)
- 2 bay leaves
- 1 teaspoon dried thyme
- Salt and black pepper to taste
- Fresh parsley for garnish

Instructions:

Brown the Lamb:
- In a large pot, heat vegetable oil over medium-high heat. Brown the lamb chunks on all sides.

Sauté Aromatics:
- Add chopped onions and minced garlic to the pot. Sauté until the onions are translucent.

Add Tomatoes and Wine:
- Stir in diced tomatoes and pour in the red wine. Allow it to simmer for a few minutes to cook off the alcohol.

Pour Broth:
- Pour in the beef or lamb broth, ensuring that it covers the lamb. Add bay leaves and dried thyme.

Simmer:
- Reduce the heat to low, cover the pot, and let the lamb simmer for about 1.5 to 2 hours or until it becomes tender.

Add Vegetables:
- Add sliced carrots, diced potatoes, and green peas to the pot. Simmer until the vegetables are cooked through.

Season:

- Season the stew with salt and black pepper to taste. Adjust the seasoning as needed.

Check Consistency:
- If the stew is too thick, you can add more broth or water to reach your desired consistency.

Garnish:
- Garnish the Ensopado de Borrego with fresh parsley before serving.

Serve:
- Serve the lamb stew hot, accompanied by crusty bread or over rice.

Angu à Baiana

Ingredients:
- 2 cups cornmeal (coarse or fine)
- 4 cups water
- 1 cup coconut milk
- 1/4 cup vegetable oil
- 1 onion, finely chopped
- 3 cloves garlic, minced
- 2 tomatoes, diced
- 1 green bell pepper, diced
- 1 red bell pepper, diced
- 1 tablespoon palm oil (dendê oil) - optional
- Salt to taste
- Fresh cilantro for garnish

Instructions:

Prepare the Cornmeal:
- In a bowl, mix the cornmeal with water until well combined. Set aside.

Sauté Aromatics:
- In a large pot, heat vegetable oil over medium heat. Add finely chopped onions and minced garlic. Sauté until the onions are translucent.

Add Vegetables:
- Stir in diced tomatoes, green bell pepper, and red bell pepper. Cook until the vegetables are softened.

Add Cornmeal Mixture:
- Pour the cornmeal mixture into the pot, stirring continuously to avoid lumps.

Cook the Cornmeal:
- Add coconut milk and palm oil (if using). Continue to stir the mixture over medium heat.

Season:
- Season with salt to taste. Continue stirring to prevent sticking to the pot.

Simmer:
- Reduce the heat to low and let the angu simmer, stirring occasionally, until it reaches a thick and creamy consistency.

Check Seasoning:
- Taste and adjust the seasoning if needed.

Garnish:

- Garnish the Angu à Baiana with fresh cilantro before serving.

Serve:
- Serve the angu hot as a side dish or as part of a traditional Bahian meal.

Angu à Baiana is a delicious cornmeal dish with the distinct flavors of Bahian cuisine, featuring coconut milk and, optionally, palm oil. It makes a flavorful accompaniment to various Brazilian dishes.

Empadão Goiano

Ingredients:

For the Dough:

- 3 cups all-purpose flour
- 1 cup unsalted butter, cold and diced
- 1 egg
- 1/4 cup cold water
- 1 teaspoon salt

For the Filling:

- 500g ground beef
- 1 onion, finely chopped
- 3 cloves garlic, minced
- 2 tomatoes, diced
- 1 cup corn kernels (fresh or frozen)
- 1 cup green peas (fresh or frozen)
- 1/2 cup black olives, sliced
- 1/2 cup green olives, sliced
- 1/2 cup fresh parsley, chopped
- 1 teaspoon ground cumin
- Salt and black pepper to taste
- 1/2 cup tomato sauce
- 1/2 cup chicken or beef broth
- 1 hard-boiled egg, sliced

Instructions:

For the Dough:

   Prepare the Dough:
   - In a large bowl, combine the flour and salt. Add the cold, diced butter and use your fingertips to rub it into the flour until it resembles breadcrumbs.

   Add Egg and Water:
   - Add the egg and cold water to the mixture. Mix until the dough comes together. If needed, add more water, a tablespoon at a time.

   Form a Disk:
   - Shape the dough into a flat disk, wrap it in plastic wrap, and refrigerate for at least 30 minutes.

For the Filling:

- Sauté Aromatics:
  - In a large skillet, sauté finely chopped onions and minced garlic until they are golden brown.
- Brown Ground Beef:
  - Add the ground beef to the skillet and cook until browned. Drain excess fat.
- Add Vegetables:
  - Stir in diced tomatoes, corn kernels, green peas, black olives, green olives, and chopped parsley.
- Season:
  - Add ground cumin, salt, and black pepper to taste. Mix well.
- Pour Sauce and Broth:
  - Pour in the tomato sauce and chicken or beef broth. Let the mixture simmer until it thickens. Remove from heat.
- Preheat Oven:
  - Preheat your oven to 350°F (180°C).
- Assemble the Pie:
  - Roll out the chilled dough on a floured surface to fit the bottom and top of your baking dish. Place the bottom layer in the dish.
- Add Filling and Egg:
  - Spoon the beef and vegetable mixture onto the dough. Place slices of hard-boiled egg on top.
- Cover with Dough:
  - Cover the filling with the remaining rolled-out dough. Seal the edges and make a few slits on the top to allow steam to escape.
- Bake:
  - Bake in the preheated oven for 35-40 minutes or until the crust is golden brown.
- Cool and Serve:
  - Allow the Empadão Goiano to cool slightly before slicing and serving.

Empadão Goiano is a hearty Brazilian dish that combines a flavorful meat and vegetable filling with a buttery and flaky crust. It's a perfect comfort food, enjoyed by many in the state of Goiás.

Pastel

Ingredients:

For the Dough:

- 3 cups all-purpose flour
- 1/2 teaspoon salt
- 1 cup warm water

For the Filling (Choose one or mix and match):

Ground Beef Filling:
- 500g ground beef
- 1 onion, finely chopped
- 2 cloves garlic, minced
- 1 tomato, diced
- 1 teaspoon ground cumin
- Salt and black pepper to taste
- Vegetable oil for cooking

Cheese Filling:
- 2 cups shredded mozzarella or your favorite melting cheese
- 1/2 cup cream cheese
- Chopped fresh parsley (optional)
- Vegetable oil for cooking

Pizza Filling:
- 1/2 cup tomato sauce
- 1 cup shredded mozzarella
- 1/4 cup sliced pepperoni or cooked sausage
- Sliced black olives (optional)
- Vegetable oil for cooking

Other Ingredients:

- Vegetable oil for deep frying

Instructions:

For the Dough:

    Make the Dough:

- In a large bowl, combine the all-purpose flour and salt. Gradually add warm water and knead until a smooth and elastic dough forms. Cover and let it rest for 30 minutes.

For the Filling:

Ground Beef Filling:
- In a pan, sauté chopped onions and minced garlic until golden. Add ground beef and cook until browned. Stir in diced tomatoes, ground cumin, salt, and black pepper. Cook until the mixture is well combined.

Cheese Filling:
- Mix shredded mozzarella with cream cheese and chopped parsley (if using).

Pizza Filling:
- Spread tomato sauce on one half of the rolled-out dough. Sprinkle shredded mozzarella, add pepperoni or sausage, and sliced olives. Fold the dough over the filling and seal the edges.

Assembling and Cooking:

Prepare Pastel:
- Divide the rested dough into small balls. Roll each ball into a thin circle or rectangle.

Add Filling:
- Place a portion of the desired filling on one half of the dough circle or rectangle.

Fold and Seal:
- Fold the other half of the dough over the filling, creating a half-moon or rectangle shape. Press the edges to seal.

Deep Fry:
- In a deep fryer or large pan, heat vegetable oil for deep frying. Carefully place the pastels in the hot oil and fry until they are golden brown.

Drain Excess Oil:
- Place the fried pastels on paper towels to drain excess oil.

Serve:
- Serve the pastels hot as a delightful snack or appetizer.

Pastel is a popular Brazilian street food known for its crispy and flaky crust with a variety of delicious fillings. You can get creative with the fillings to suit your taste preferences. Enjoy!

Sagu de Vinho

Ingredients:

- 1 cup small tapioca pearls (sagu)
- 2 cups red wine (choose a sweet red wine)
- 1 cup water
- 1 cup sugar
- 1 cinnamon stick
- Zest of one orange (optional)
- Fresh fruit for garnish (such as grapes or berries)

Instructions:

Soak Tapioca Pearls:
- Rinse the tapioca pearls under cold water. In a bowl, soak them in the red wine for at least 2 hours or overnight. Make sure the tapioca pearls are fully submerged.

Cook Tapioca:
- In a saucepan, combine the soaked tapioca pearls along with the wine, water, sugar, cinnamon stick, and orange zest (if using).

Bring to a Boil:
- Bring the mixture to a boil over medium heat, stirring constantly to prevent sticking.

Simmer:
- Reduce the heat to low and let the mixture simmer, stirring occasionally, until the tapioca pearls become translucent and the pudding thickens. This may take about 15-20 minutes.

Remove Cinnamon Stick:
- Once the tapioca pearls are cooked, remove the cinnamon stick.

Cool:
- Allow the Sagu de Vinho to cool to room temperature. It will continue to thicken as it cools.

Chill (Optional):
- You can chill the pudding in the refrigerator for a few hours if you prefer it cold.

Serve:
- Serve the Sagu de Vinho in individual bowls or glasses, garnished with fresh fruit.

Enjoy:

- Enjoy this delightful wine-infused tapioca pudding, a popular Brazilian dessert with a unique and rich flavor.

Sagu de Vinho is a traditional Brazilian dessert, and the use of red wine gives it a distinctive taste. It's a sweet and comforting treat that is often served at special occasions and celebrations.

Maria Isabel

Ingredients:

- 2 cups cooked rice
- 500g shredded cooked beef (leftover roast beef works well)
- 1 onion, finely chopped
- 3 cloves garlic, minced
- 2 tomatoes, diced
- 1 green bell pepper, diced
- 1 red bell pepper, diced
- 2 tablespoons vegetable oil
- 1 cup green peas (fresh or frozen)
- 1 cup corn kernels (fresh or frozen)
- 2 hard-boiled eggs, sliced
- Salt and black pepper to taste
- Fresh parsley for garnish

Instructions:

Prepare Ingredients:
- Ensure that the rice and beef are cooked and ready. Shred the cooked beef into small pieces.

Sauté Aromatics:
- In a large pan, heat vegetable oil over medium-high heat. Add finely chopped onions and minced garlic. Sauté until the onions are translucent.

Add Peppers and Tomatoes:
- Stir in diced green and red bell peppers, and diced tomatoes. Cook until the vegetables are softened.

Add Shredded Beef:
- Add the shredded cooked beef to the pan. Mix well with the sautéed vegetables.

Incorporate Rice:
- Add the cooked rice to the pan, combining it with the beef and vegetable mixture.

Add Peas and Corn:
- Mix in green peas and corn kernels. Stir until all ingredients are well distributed.

Season:

- Season the Maria Isabel with salt and black pepper to taste. Adjust the seasoning as needed.

Simmer:
- Let the mixture simmer for a few minutes to allow the flavors to meld. Ensure everything is heated through.

Garnish:
- Garnish the Maria Isabel with sliced hard-boiled eggs and fresh parsley.

Serve:
- Serve the Maria Isabel hot, either as a standalone dish or as a side to other Brazilian specialties.

Maria Isabel is a flavorful Brazilian dish that combines rice, shredded beef, and a medley of vegetables. It's a hearty and comforting meal that reflects the diverse and delicious nature of Brazilian cuisine.

Cocido Brasileño

Ingredients:

For the Broth:

- 1 kg beef shank or brisket, bone-in
- 1 kg pork ribs or pork belly
- 1 large onion, peeled and halved
- 4 cloves garlic, peeled
- 2 carrots, peeled and chopped
- 2 celery stalks, chopped
- 1 leek, cleaned and chopped
- 1 bay leaf
- Salt to taste

For the Vegetables and Legumes:

- 2 sweet potatoes, peeled and cubed
- 2 plantains, peeled and sliced
- 2 ears of corn, shucked and halved
- 2 potatoes, peeled and diced
- 2 cassava roots, peeled and sliced
- 2 zucchinis, sliced
- 1 cabbage, quartered
- 1 bunch kale or collard greens, stems removed and leaves chopped
- 1 cup green beans, trimmed
- 1 cup peas (fresh or frozen)
- Salt and pepper to taste

Instructions:

For the Broth:

> Prepare the Meat:
> - In a large pot, place the beef shank or brisket, pork ribs or pork belly, onion halves, garlic cloves, carrots, celery, leek, and bay leaf.
>
> Add Water:
> - Fill the pot with enough water to cover the ingredients. Add salt to taste.
>
> Bring to a Boil:

- Bring the broth to a boil, then reduce the heat to simmer. Skim off any foam that rises to the surface.

Simmer:
- Simmer the broth for at least 2-3 hours, allowing the meat to become tender and the flavors to meld. Add more water if needed.

Strain the Broth:
- Once the broth is rich and flavorful, strain it to remove the solids, leaving only the clear broth.

For the Vegetables and Legumes:

Prepare Vegetables:
- In a separate pot, place the sweet potatoes, plantains, corn, potatoes, cassava, zucchinis, cabbage, kale or collard greens, green beans, and peas.

Add Broth:
- Pour the strained broth over the vegetables, ensuring they are fully submerged. Add salt and pepper to taste.

Simmer Vegetables:
- Simmer the vegetables until they are tender. The cooking time may vary for each type of vegetable, so add them gradually.

Serve:
- Once the vegetables are cooked, serve the Cocido Brasileño hot. You can arrange the meats and vegetables on a large platter or serve them in individual bowls.

Cocido Brasileño is a hearty and nourishing dish that brings together a variety of meats, vegetables, and legumes in a flavorful broth. It's a comforting meal, perfect for gatherings and celebrations.

Dobradinha

Ingredients:

- 500g tripe, cleaned and cut into small pieces
- 1 cup white beans, soaked overnight
- 2 tablespoons vegetable oil
- 1 large onion, finely chopped
- 4 cloves garlic, minced
- 2 tomatoes, diced
- 1 bell pepper, diced
- 2 chorizo sausages, sliced
- 200g smoked sausage (linguiça defumada), sliced
- 1 bay leaf
- 1 teaspoon ground cumin
- 1 teaspoon paprika
- Salt and black pepper to taste
- Fresh parsley for garnish
- Lime wedges for serving

Instructions:

Prepare Tripe and Beans:
- Clean the tripe thoroughly and cut it into small pieces. Soak the white beans overnight.

Cook Beans:
- In a large pot, cook the soaked white beans until they are tender. Drain and set aside.

Boil Tripe:
- Boil the tripe in a separate pot until it becomes tender. This may take about 1-2 hours. Drain and set aside.

Sauté Aromatics:
- In a large pan, heat vegetable oil over medium heat. Add finely chopped onions and minced garlic. Sauté until the onions are translucent.

Add Tomatoes and Peppers:
- Stir in diced tomatoes and bell pepper. Cook until the vegetables are softened.

Combine Meats:
- Add the boiled tripe, cooked white beans, sliced chorizo sausages, and sliced smoked sausage to the pan. Mix well.

Season:
- Season the mixture with a bay leaf, ground cumin, paprika, salt, and black pepper. Adjust the seasoning to taste.

Simmer:
- Let the Dobradinha simmer over low heat for about 30-40 minutes, allowing the flavors to meld.

Check Consistency:
- Check the consistency of the dish. If it's too dry, you can add a bit of water.

Garnish:
- Garnish the Dobradinha with fresh parsley.

Serve:
- Serve the Dobradinha hot, accompanied by lime wedges for squeezing over the top.

Dobradinha is a traditional Brazilian dish made with tripe and beans, cooked with a flavorful blend of spices and sausages. It's a hearty and satisfying dish that reflects the rich culinary diversity of Brazilian cuisine.

Canjica Nordestina

Ingredients:

- 2 cups white corn (canjica), soaked overnight
- 1 cup coconut milk
- 1 cup whole milk
- 1 cup sugar
- 1 cinnamon stick
- 3 cloves
- 1 can (400g) sweetened condensed milk
- 1 cup coconut flakes (optional)
- Ground cinnamon for garnish

Instructions:

Soak Canjica:
- Rinse the white corn (canjica) under cold water and soak it in water overnight.

Cook Canjica:
- In a large pot, add the soaked canjica with enough water to cover it. Bring it to a boil, then reduce the heat to simmer until the canjica becomes tender. This may take about 1-2 hours. Drain any excess water.

Prepare Coconut Milk Mixture:
- In a separate saucepan, combine coconut milk, whole milk, sugar, cinnamon stick, and cloves. Heat the mixture over medium heat, stirring until the sugar is dissolved.

Combine Canjica and Coconut Milk Mixture:
- Add the cooked canjica to the coconut milk mixture. Stir well and let it simmer over low heat for about 15-20 minutes, allowing the flavors to meld.

Add Sweetened Condensed Milk:
- Pour in the sweetened condensed milk, stirring continuously to achieve a creamy consistency.

Optional Coconut Flakes:
- If using coconut flakes, add them to the mixture and stir until well combined. This adds an extra layer of texture and flavor.

Simmer:
- Continue to simmer the Canjica Nordestina until it reaches your desired thickness.

Check Sweetness:
- Taste and adjust the sweetness by adding more sugar or sweetened condensed milk if needed.

Remove Whole Spices:
- Remove the cinnamon stick and cloves from the mixture.

Serve Warm or Cold:
- Canjica Nordestina can be served warm or chilled. If serving it chilled, refrigerate it for a few hours.

Garnish and Enjoy:
- Before serving, sprinkle ground cinnamon on top for garnish. Serve the Canjica Nordestina and enjoy this delightful Brazilian dessert.

Canjica Nordestina is a creamy and sweet corn pudding infused with coconut and spices, commonly enjoyed as a traditional dessert in the northeastern region of Brazil. It's particularly popular during festive occasions and celebrations.

Caruru

Ingredients:

- 1 cup okra, finely chopped
- 1 cup dried shrimp, soaked in water and drained
- 1 cup peanuts, toasted and ground
- 1 cup finely chopped onion
- 1 cup finely chopped tomatoes
- 1 cup finely chopped bell pepper (green or red)
- 1 cup chopped fresh cilantro
- 1 cup chopped fresh parsley
- 1 cup palm oil (dendê oil)
- 2 tablespoons ground crayfish
- 2 tablespoons ground peanuts (for extra thickness)
- 2 tablespoons ground dried shrimp
- 2 cloves garlic, minced
- 1 teaspoon ground ginger
- 1 teaspoon ground chili pepper (adjust to taste)
- Salt to taste
- Cooked white rice for serving

Instructions:

Prepare Ingredients:
- Finely chop okra, onions, tomatoes, bell pepper, fresh cilantro, fresh parsley, and mince garlic.

Prepare Dried Shrimp:
- Soak dried shrimp in water for about 30 minutes, then drain.

Toast Peanuts:
- Toast peanuts in a dry pan until golden, then grind them into a coarse powder.

Prepare Palm Oil:
- Heat palm oil in a large pot. Be cautious, as palm oil stains easily. If you prefer, you can heat the palm oil in a separate pan and then add it to the pot.

Sauté Aromatics:
- Sauté chopped onions, minced garlic, ground ginger, and ground chili pepper in the palm oil until the onions are translucent.

Add Okra:

- Add the finely chopped okra to the pot. Stir well and cook for a few minutes until the okra is slightly tender.

Add Tomatoes and Bell Pepper:
- Add chopped tomatoes and bell pepper. Cook until they are softened.

Add Dried Shrimp and Ground Crayfish:
- Stir in soaked and drained dried shrimp, ground crayfish, and ground dried shrimp.

Add Ground Peanuts:
- Add the ground peanuts to the pot for thickness. Stir well to combine.

Add Toasted Peanuts:
- Add the toasted and ground peanuts to the pot. Mix thoroughly.

Season:
- Season the Caruru with salt to taste. Adjust the seasoning as needed.

Finish with Fresh Herbs:
- Add chopped fresh cilantro and fresh parsley to the pot. Stir and let the Caruru simmer for a few more minutes.

Serve:
- Serve the Caruru over cooked white rice.

Caruru is a traditional Brazilian dish with African roots, known for its rich and flavorful combination of okra, dried shrimp, peanuts, and spices. It's often served during festivities and celebrations. Enjoy this unique and delicious dish!

Canjica com Amendoim

Ingredients:

- 1 cup white corn (canjica), soaked overnight
- 1 cup roasted peanuts, coarsely ground
- 1 cup sweetened condensed milk
- 1 cup coconut milk
- 1 cup whole milk
- 1 cup sugar
- 1 cinnamon stick
- 3 cloves
- Pinch of salt
- Ground cinnamon for garnish (optional)

Instructions:

Soak Canjica:
- Rinse the white corn (canjica) under cold water and soak it in water overnight.

Boil Canjica:
- In a large pot, add the soaked canjica with enough water to cover it. Bring it to a boil, then reduce the heat to simmer until the canjica becomes tender. This may take about 1-2 hours. Drain any excess water.

Prepare Peanut Mixture:
- While the canjica is cooking, roast peanuts in a dry pan until golden. Coarsely grind the roasted peanuts.

Combine Ingredients:
- In a separate pot, combine sweetened condensed milk, coconut milk, whole milk, sugar, cinnamon stick, cloves, and a pinch of salt. Heat the mixture over medium heat, stirring until the sugar is dissolved.

Add Canjica and Peanuts:
- Add the cooked canjica to the milk mixture. Stir well and let it simmer over low heat for about 15-20 minutes, allowing the flavors to meld.

Add Ground Peanuts:
- Stir in the coarsely ground roasted peanuts. Mix well to incorporate the peanuts into the mixture.

Simmer:
- Continue to simmer the Canjica com Amendoim until it reaches your desired thickness.

Check Sweetness:
- Taste and adjust the sweetness by adding more sugar or sweetened condensed milk if needed.

Remove Whole Spices:
- Remove the cinnamon stick and cloves from the mixture.

Serve Warm or Cold:
- Canjica com Amendoim can be served warm or chilled. If serving it chilled, refrigerate it for a few hours.

Garnish and Enjoy:
- Before serving, sprinkle ground cinnamon on top for garnish if desired. Serve the Canjica com Amendoim and enjoy this delightful Brazilian dessert.

Canjica com Amendoim is a delicious and creamy Brazilian dessert that combines the richness of peanuts with the sweetness of canjica. It's often enjoyed during festivities and special occasions.

Bolo de Rolo

Ingredients:

For the Cake Batter:

- 4 large eggs
- 1 cup granulated sugar
- 1 cup all-purpose flour
- 1 teaspoon vanilla extract
- Green food coloring (optional)

For the Guava Paste Filling:

- 1 1/2 cups guava paste, melted and cooled

For Rolling:

- Powdered sugar for dusting

Instructions:

Cake Batter:

> Preheat Oven:
> - Preheat your oven to 350°F (180°C). Grease and line a jelly roll pan or a baking sheet with parchment paper.
>
> Prepare Eggs and Sugar:
> - In a large bowl, beat the eggs and granulated sugar together until light and fluffy. This can take about 5-7 minutes.
>
> Add Vanilla Extract:
> - Mix in the vanilla extract.
>
> Fold in Flour:
> - Gently fold in the all-purpose flour until well combined. Be careful not to deflate the batter.
>
> Add Food Coloring (Optional):
> - If desired, add green food coloring to achieve the traditional color of Bolo de Rolo.
>
> Spread Batter:
> - Spread the batter evenly onto the prepared jelly roll pan.
>
> Bake:

- Bake in the preheated oven for approximately 8-10 minutes or until the cake is just set.

Guava Paste Filling:

Prepare Guava Paste:
- While the cake is baking, melt the guava paste in a saucepan over low heat. Allow it to cool.

Assembly:

Roll the Cake:
- Once the cake is baked, immediately invert it onto a clean kitchen towel dusted with powdered sugar.

Remove Parchment Paper:
- Carefully peel off the parchment paper from the back of the cake.

Spread Guava Paste:
- Spread the melted guava paste evenly over the warm cake.

Roll the Cake:
- Starting from the shorter end, carefully roll the cake with the guava paste into a tight log. Use the kitchen towel to help you roll it evenly.

Cool:
- Allow the rolled cake to cool completely.

Slice and Serve:
- Once cooled, slice the Bolo de Rolo into rounds and serve. The spiral pattern of guava paste will be revealed in each slice.

Bolo de Rolo is a Brazilian rolled sponge cake with a sweet guava paste filling. It's a beautiful and delicious treat often enjoyed as a dessert or during special occasions.

Bolo de Rolo

Ingredients:

For the Cake Batter:

- 4 large eggs
- 1 cup granulated sugar
- 1 cup all-purpose flour
- 1 teaspoon vanilla extract
- Green food coloring (optional)

For the Guava Paste Filling:

- 1 1/2 cups guava paste, melted and cooled

For Rolling:

- Powdered sugar for dusting

Instructions:

Cake Batter:

　Preheat Oven:
- Preheat your oven to 350°F (180°C). Grease and line a jelly roll pan or a baking sheet with parchment paper.

　Prepare Eggs and Sugar:
- In a large bowl, beat the eggs and granulated sugar together until light and fluffy. This can take about 5-7 minutes.

　Add Vanilla Extract:
- Mix in the vanilla extract.

　Fold in Flour:
- Gently fold in the all-purpose flour until well combined. Be careful not to deflate the batter.

　Add Food Coloring (Optional):
- If desired, add green food coloring to achieve the traditional color of Bolo de Rolo.

　Spread Batter:
- Spread the batter evenly onto the prepared jelly roll pan.

　Bake:

- Bake in the preheated oven for approximately 8-10 minutes or until the cake is just set.

Guava Paste Filling:

Prepare Guava Paste:
- While the cake is baking, melt the guava paste in a saucepan over low heat. Allow it to cool.

Assembly:

Roll the Cake:
- Once the cake is baked, immediately invert it onto a clean kitchen towel dusted with powdered sugar.

Remove Parchment Paper:
- Carefully peel off the parchment paper from the back of the cake.

Spread Guava Paste:
- Spread the melted guava paste evenly over the warm cake.

Roll the Cake:
- Starting from the shorter end, carefully roll the cake with the guava paste into a tight log. Use the kitchen towel to help you roll it evenly.

Cool:
- Allow the rolled cake to cool completely.

Slice and Serve:
- Once cooled, slice the Bolo de Rolo into rounds and serve. The spiral pattern of guava paste will be revealed in each slice.

Bolo de Rolo is a Brazilian rolled sponge cake with a sweet guava paste filling. It's a beautiful and delicious treat often enjoyed as a dessert or during special occasions.